The Barefoot Book of

HEROINES

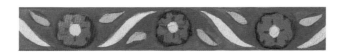

The Barefoot Book of

HEROINES

Written and Illustrated by Rebecca Hazell

BAREFOOT BOOKS

BATH

Contents

To Doris Knotts, my mother and a true heroine

Barefoot Collections
an imprint of
Barefoot Books
PO Box 95
Kingswood
Bristol
BS30 5BH

Graphic design by Design/Section, Frome
Printed and bound in Hong Kong by South China Printing Co. (1988) Ltd
This book has been printed on 100% acid-free paper

Hardcover ISBN 1 898000 87 5
Paperback ISBN 1 84148 200 5

British Cataloguing-in-Publication Data: a catalogue record
for this book is available from the British Library

1 3 5 7 9 8 6 4 2

Acknowledgements

Thank you to my wonderful husband Mark, who helped me in untold ways, and to my children, Elisabeth and Stephan, who had to re-read these stories until we were all happy with them. Also, thank you to Trudy Sable, Ruth Whitehead, Gillian Webster, Bill Gilkerson, Sam Bercholz, Deborah Luscomb and all my friends who helped with books and advice. I want to express my appreciation to all the artists (and photographers) from ancient times to the present, who left a record of their world for us to share. I relied on them to show me how to picture what life was like for each heroine. Thank you, Clea Derwent, for suggesting this book. Many thanks to my excellent editor, Tessa Strickland, and to Pamela Dix, my thoroughgoing copy-editor.

*The self-portrait of Frida Kahlo appearing on page 77
is reproduced courtesy of Albright-Knox Art Gallery, Buffalo,
New York, Bequest of A. Conger Goodyear, 1966.*

Introduction

When I was young, my mother gave me a special book. It was a guided tour to all the most wonderful places in the world. The author not only described the places, he brought the people who had lived there back to life. A lot of his stories were about women.

Now that I'm grown up, I know that my storyteller added details that were from his imagination. Still, he woke up my own imagination, and I have loved history ever since. I also know now that history is full of people and events that are more astonishing than any made-up story. What people have done and achieved is so amazing that I want to share some of their stories with you. The stories are all true, and they are all about heroines.

When we think of heroism, we may imagine dramatic rescues and daring deeds, and think of famous war heroes, or picture someone risking his or her life to save someone wounded or in danger. These kinds of heroism don't happen every day.

Other kinds of heroism last for a lifetime. Some people lead heroic lives by being brave or kind, and others are heroic because of their ability to see or do things in a new way. The women you will meet in this book were brave, kind or visionary, and sometimes all three. They embraced their lives and lived them fully, and they all gave something to the world around them.

Some of these heroines were very unpopular in their time. They made mistakes, just like we do. They were not perfect, but they were so full of life. You will meet different kinds of heroines from all over the world and from different times in history. I couldn't include heroines from every country, though there are heroic people everywhere. I am sure you know of a few who should be here, and I wish they were, too. Still, you will see many of the things women have done and been – from queens to slaves, from artists to doctors.

Of course there were many heroes in history too, and ideally this book would include them also. But heroines have often been overlooked, and we need to know about their place in our histories too. One day, heroes and heroines will appear side by side in every history book. Until then, ladies first, as one of our heroines would have said.

I have used different styles to illustrate the book, to show the artistic style of the particular period and place in which each heroine lived. I hope you enjoy these glimpses into their lives, and that you see a bit of yourself in each one of them.

Rebecca Hazell

Agnodice

Between the sixth and fourth century BC, a remarkable civilisation flourished in Greece, home to gifted doctors, men and women. From ancient times, the women of Greece had been healers. They had to know how to deliver babies, take care of their mothers, sisters and friends and heal their children's cuts and bruises. They also had to take care of men injured in peace and in war. Every woman had to know something about healing.

However, by Agnodice's time (from around 450 to 300 BC) women were losing their place of respect in Greece, not only in medicine but in society in general. By the fourth century BC, doctors were generally men. Women were no longer welcome as professional healers.

Agnodice lived in the city-state of Athens. Women were not considered important enough to have their birth and death dates recorded, so we don't know exactly when she lived. We only know about her through ancient stories, some of which are legends.

Agnodice was inspired to risk condemnation and become a doctor. It can't have been easy to find a teacher. She studied under a famous open-minded doctor named Herophilus. She learned his formulae for making medicines from herbs and minerals. More importantly, she learned how to perform surgery, especially for women's ailments. Once she was on her own, she mostly took care of women.

Because women weren't supposed to practise medicine, Agnodice dressed as a man. Her disguise was discovered somehow, and she got into trouble. She proudly admitted to being a woman once she was discovered and put on trial. It isn't clear which was worse to the men of Athens – her dressing in men's clothes or practising medicine!

Either way, her loyal patients came to her rescue. Wives and mothers threatened to go on strike unless she was freed. Their arguments must have been powerful, because she was released right away. Not only that, she could now practise medicine and dress however she chose.

Agnodice's story doesn't tell us whether she went back to wearing women's clothing. I like to think she did, once she no longer needed to hide who she was. Agnodice continued her medical practice, passing into legend as a symbol of capable womanhood.

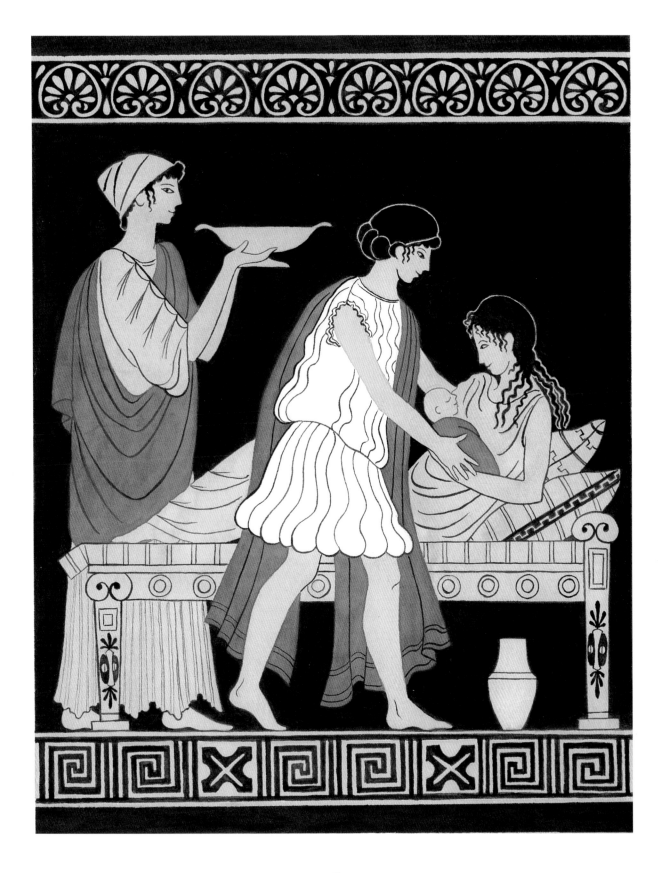

DIVINE HEALERS

In ancient times, people didn't distinguish between legendary heroes and historical figures. Both in Egypt and Greece, outstanding people sometimes passed into legend. Agnodice was such a heroine. Other heroes even became 'sainted mortals' as time passed, with gods and goddesses for parents.

In Greece, the family of Asclepius, Hygieia and Panacea may have been sainted mortals. If so, these famous healers would have lived about 900 BC. The great god Apollo was supposedly the father of Asclepius, who became the patron god of medicine. Hygieia became the goddess of prevention and Panacea the goddess of curing. Even today, we practice 'hygiene' – healthy habits that prevent disease. Panacea now means a universal cure.

Brightly painted statues stood in the temples of Hygieia, Asklepios and Panacea.

The ancient doctor's pledge, called the Hippocratic Oath, began, 'I swear by Apollo the physician, by Asclepius, by Hygieia and Panacea and by all the gods and goddesses making them my witness, that I will fulfill according to my ability and judgment this oath and this covenant.' Agnodice might have taken this pledge. Today, new doctors still take a form of the Hippocratic Oath, committing themselves to helping others.

For centuries after Agnodice, women in medicine were rare. Sometimes their achievements went unrecorded, or men got credit for them. Around 100 AD a Greek named Metrodora wrote the oldest surviving medical text composed by a woman. No one believed a woman could have written it, so for centuries it was credited to 'Metrodorus', a man's name. A few outstanding women of medicine did become famous. One was Hildegard of Bingen, a German abbess who lived in the twelfth century. In addition to having visions, composing music, running two convents and advising people like Queen Eleanor of Aquitaine, Hildegard wrote a book inspired by her visions. It listed the causes and cures for disease. Some of her intuitions, such as the way blood circulates, were correct and far ahead of her time.

Still, it wasn't until the nineteenth century that women could become fully trained doctors again. Some exceptional women in the field of medicine include Nobel Prize winners such as Marie Curie (Radiology), Dorothy Hodgkin (Chemistry) and Rosalyn Yalow (Medicine/Physiology). Nowadays, more and more women are medical professionals. From family doctors to pioneering researchers, women are contributing to the future of medicine.

AGNODICE'S WORLD

If Agnodice lived in the fourth or third century BC, she would have seen Athens slowly decline in power from an empire to a subject state. But despite political woes, in philosophy, art, science and medicine Athens was the queen of cities.

The city-state of Athens was famous for its learned and creative people. The city was dominated by a great hill called the Acropolis, where fine marble temples stood, honouring Athens' patroness Athena, goddess of wisdom.

Below the Acropolis, the city spread around a large central meeting area called the Agora. Used for sports, public meetings, trade and trials, this would have been the place where Agnodice

The patron goddess of Athens was Athena, whose totem animal was an owl, symbolizing wisdom.

was brought for judgment. She was not alone in being tried unjustly. In 399 BC, the leaders of Athens tried and convicted the great Socrates, father of Western philosophy. He was condemned to drink poison for corrupting the youth of Athens with his ideas.

Despite its political struggles, Athens would have been an exciting place to live. Perhaps Agnodice listened to speeches by the city's famous statesman Pericles, and saw plays by the comic playwright Aristophanes. Athens was also home to Socrates' heir, Plato. The great doctor Hippocrates lived in the third century BC and travelled to Athens, where Agnodice may have met him.

We can imagine Agnodice after her trial, striding proudly through the Agora, while the women she treated waited for her in seclusion. Athenian women did not go out much. Perhaps she told them about what was going on in the world outside, a world she was now free to enter. Perhaps she simply tended their injuries or fevers, or delivered a baby, rejoicing with them when it took its first breath.

GREECE IN THE 6TH-4TH CENTURY BC

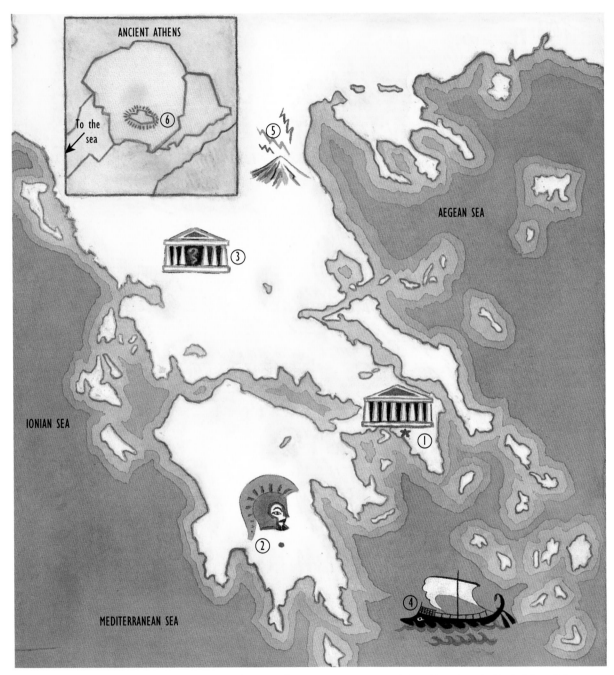

1. Agnodice's home was in Athens, which dominated the city states of Greece politically and culturally.

2. Athens' rival and enemy, Sparta, finally overcame Athens.

3. Temples devoted to Asclepius and his attendant daughters once stood all over Greece. They were places of healing and dreams, and home to sacred snakes.

4. Hippocrates sailed to Athens from the island of Kos, which was Asclepius' home too.

5. Mount Olympus was where all the Greek gods were thought to live, ruled by Athena's father, Zeus.

6. Inset: Athens in the fifth century BC.

 Lady Murasaki Shikibu

About 1000 years ago, a noble Japanese lady served at the Imperial court in Kyoto. She did not use her real name, so we know her as Lady Murasaki Shikibu. 'Murasaki' means lavender; it was the name of one of the heroines in *The Tale of Genji*. The world's first novel, *The Tale of Genji* was a romance about Prince Genji, his sons and the ladies they loved. In it Lady Murasaki created a lasting picture of her world and people. Even the original copies of this novel are long gone – the oldest copies date from centuries later.

The Japanese court was formal and refined. Beyond ceremonial duties and rules of polite behaviour, people's lives centred around poetry, music, calligraphy and each other. Young ladies were kept isolated from gentlemen, which made them seem highly attractive to the young men who pursued them. They wrote poetic notes and played music to their mysterious ladies, who remained hidden behind curtains and screens. If they were lucky, the ladies would write back and play music for them, too. Sometimes they would even arrange secret meetings.

However, *The Tale of Genji* was not just a romance – it is one of the greatest novels ever written in any language. Lady Murasaki described how her characters felt and how they changed with time, bringing her story to life with details like the sound of crickets, the rustle of silks and the aroma of perfume. She also showed that living in a world of grace and refinement did not keep people from suffering. Lady Murasaki presented life as fascinating and yet fleeting, and her writing showed a deep appreciation of beauty.

The Tale of Genji has been translated into many languages, and people around the world still enjoy reading it. Lady Murasaki herself remains a mystery, but she gave us an enduring picture of a world long gone.

MEDIEVAL JAPANESE CULTURE

Lady Murasaki lived in a special time. For 200 years, Japan had absorbed the culture and arts of its great neighbour, China. Now it could look with pride on its own traditions. In architecture, art, textiles, music, dance and literature, the Japanese were finding new and exciting ways to express themselves. These traditions were not limited to court people, but spread throughout Japan. Compared to medieval Europe, Japan was a very civilised place to live.

Court lords and ladies liked to write, usually little poems or books about their enjoyment of nature. Even famous warriors had to be good poets. Some works have survived, like *The Pillow Book*, which described one lady's thoughts under categories like 'Amusing Things' and 'Annoying Things'. Lady Murasaki, however, was the first person to tell a full-length story about realistic characters.

While a 'cloistered' Emperor managed politics from behind the scenes...

In *The Tale of Genji*, Lady Murasaki used the Japanese language in a new way that expressed rich and powerful images. It was full of double meanings and puns. For instance, the word for pine tree in Japanese is the same as 'to wait', so when she mentioned pines, she implied a sense of longing for a loved one. (We also talk about 'pining' for a loved one.) Lady Murasaki's writing could be funny or sad, but it captured part of the Japanese spirit, which sees beauty and sorrow together, and it continues to influence Japanese literature even today.

The Tale of Genji also inspired Japanese art. Around that time, artists began painting scrolls with a series of pictures that told a story. People read the scrolls in the same way as reading a comic strip. At first there was writing to describe the action, but soon the words became unnecessary. Instead, each picture was separated from the next by clouds or mountains. With the story in picture form, everyone could follow it, even if they could not read. The oldest known picture scroll is of *The Tale of Genji*.

...young ladies managed courtship from behind screens.

DETAILS FROM A LADY'S LIFE

Lady Murasaki was probably born around 978. Shikibu was a rank, possibly held by her father. Her father was governor of a province, and she may have travelled with him just before she married. Soon after marrying she had a daughter, and was then widowed. Around 1005 she came to serve at court. She kept a diary from 1007 to 1010, in which she recalled her dead husband, General Fujiwara Nobutaka, and described serving the Empress Joto Mon'in. She probably died in 1015, when she was still in her thirties.

Lady Murasaki's family was part of the powerful Fujiwara clan, which had gained control over the government of Japan, partly by marrying their women to the emperors and other powerful nobles. By Lady Murasaki's time, the Fujiwaras were the emperors. One emperor had wearied of the pomp and ceremony of court life. Retiring early, he gave up the throne to his son, to run things from behind the scenes. However, his son also decided to retire from public life, and gave up the throne to his brother. This brother also retired early, with the result that several retired emperors were trying to run things at the same time! Lady Murasaki made these Fujiwara marriage and retirement practices part of her story.

Meanwhile the ladies had their own customs, which Lady Murasaki also described. Knowing that their marriages had great political importance, they painted their eyebrows and teeth black for beauty, and wore perfumed silks. Their glossy dark hair grew so long it touched the floor. They also mastered the arts of music and elegant poetry. All this was to attract powerful nobles for husbands. Some, though, also gossiped and tried to cause trouble for others.

We can imagine Lady Murasaki, dressed as elegantly as the other ladies, watching and listening to everything around her. Instead of joining in the gossip, she writes a story that is as real as her own world. She lets a few friends read it, and they tell their friends about it. They want copies of it, too. As more people read and copy it, her fame spreads. Her book began as a pastime, but Lady Murasaki ended up changing Japanese literature forever.

JAPAN, 1000 YEARS AGO

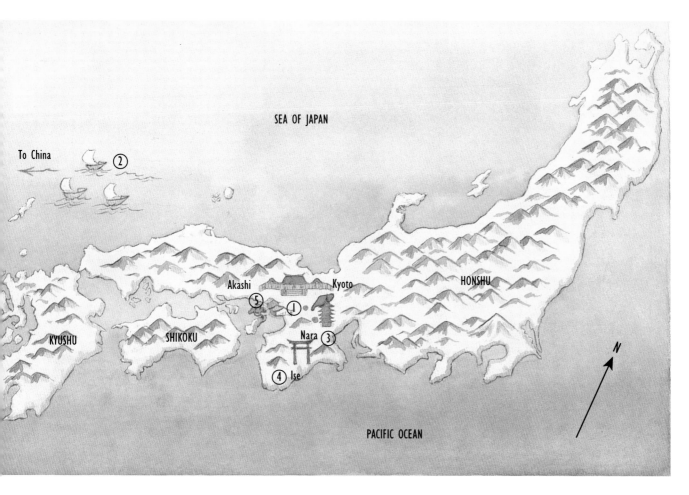

1. In Lady Murasaki's time, Kyoto was called Heian-kyo. Many of the streets mentioned in Genji are still there.

2. Over 200 years before Murasaki Shikibu lived, Japanese ships had sailed to China to learn about its culture.

3. The Fujiwaras abandoned the early capital of Nara, but many ancient Buddhist shrines still stand there. Lady Murasaki may have visited them.

4. The major Shinto shrine was at Ise. One of Genji's ladies was chief priestess there. Shinto shrines are entered by gates called torii.

5. Another spot where Genji lived when out of favour at court is now a city called Akashi.

Eleanor *of* Aquitaine

In 1137, a beautiful fifteen-year-old inherited the lands of Aquitaine, in what is now France. Aquitaine and Duchess Eleanor were both prizes, and young King Louis VII immediately married her, so doubling the size of France. Marriage was seen as an alliance between royal or noble families, not a love match.

Her new home in Paris seemed dull to the fun-loving young queen. Louis' people disapproved of her. Eager to escape, she joined Louis on the Second Crusade as armies formed across Europe, marching to take Jesus Christ's homeland from the Turks. Partly due to Louis' poor leadership, the Crusade ended disastrously. With thousands dead, Eleanor began to despise him. Then gossip spread about her. As Louis was deeply religious, only a devil could have caused his failure: high-spirited Eleanor must be that devil.

Back in France, Eleanor wanted a divorce. In those days, women never divorced men, although men could divorce women. Louis finally agreed, though it meant losing Aquitaine. Eleanor was now twenty-eight years old. She soon married King Henry II of England, starting a new life. Her royal seal showed her holding a falcon for England and a fleur-de-lis for Aquitaine, to symbolize their union. At first, Henry let Eleanor help him rule, and she often travelled with him over their domains. At other times she stood in for him when he was away. She was a just and capable ruler. But after she had borne him eight children, Henry lost interest in her.

A disappointed Eleanor returned to Aquitaine and governed alone. She was a patron of art, music and poetry, and taught her knights manners, creating the first 'gentlemen'. She commissioned a guidebook on courting a lady. This influence slowly spread across Europe, improving respect for women.

This happy time ended when Eleanor supported her sons' revolt against Henry. He imprisoned her in England until his death sixteen years later. When their son Richard the Lion Heart became king, he left his kingdom in Eleanor's care to go on the Third Crusade. She kept her younger son John from usurping the throne, and ransomed Richard from kidnappers.

Eleanor became the 'grandmother of Europe'. Her descendants included famous kings and queens like Queen Isabella of Spain and a saint, Louis IX. She had ruled as well as the strongest monarchs of her time, and her influence is still felt by us today. Whenever a man stands up to greet a woman or opens a door for her, he is one of Eleanor's 'gentlemen'.

THE FEUDAL WORLD

In Eleanor's time, the men of Europe thought of both their domains and their wives as property. As 'daughters' of Eve, the first woman, they were thought to have caused the downfall of men (just as Eleanor 'caused' Louis' failure in the Crusade). Their duty was to obey their husbands and have sons. They could own property, but men controlled it. But Eleanor frightened and angered many conservatives of her time, because she insisted on being more than property, proving she was as competent as any man.

Eleanor lived in the era of feudalism, a pyramid system of society. At the bottom were peasants, who gave goods and service to their overlords in return for protection. Their lords were 'vassals' to greater overlords. Knights were vassals to barons, and so on through count and duke, king and emperor.

A knight pledges loyalty to his lord.

A man with a good horse could become a chevalier, or knight. Chivalry comes from the French word cheval, meaning horse. Though chivalry meant honour and gallantry, many hot-headed young knights and barons fought for their own amusement, destroying property and killing innocent people. Strong rulers like Henry II and Eleanor of Aquitaine, however, controlled their vassals and protected their people.

Feudalism caused Europe many problems. For instance, King Henry and Queen Eleanor were both vassals of the King of France, which meant that France and England were tied politically even after Louis divorced Eleanor. Naturally there were bitter feelings between them. Other royal intermarriages caused similar tangles of allegiances and rival claims to thrones.

One unifying force in Europe was Christianity, with the clergy trying to keep peace and promote virtue. The Crusades began as a way to link rival kings and knights in a common cause. But the clergy was always divided in its opinion of Eleanor – her independence seemed to threaten society.

THE TROUBADOURS

Were all the world mine
from the sea to the Rhine
I'd give it away
if the English Queen
would love me one day.
Anonymous, mid-twelfth century

Troubadours took the symbols of the knightly pledge and turned them into symbols of love.

Eleanor of Aquitaine inspired love as well as hatred. This poet and many like him loved and admired her. In a time when war was a sport and women were possessions, she tried to encourage love, gentleness, courtesy and respect for women.

Eleanor had grown up in a more refined world than that of Louis or Henry. Her idea of romance was love freely given, something rare in marriages of her time. Eleanor's grandfather was a founder of the troubadour tradition. Troubadours wrote love songs and poetry. In the past, song and poetry had celebrated great battles and warlike qualities like honour and bravery, the world of chivalry. The troubadours offered a view of life in which tenderness and an appreciation of beauty mattered – the world of courtliness and romantic love.

Aquitaine was a centre for the troubadour tradition, where Eleanor passed on her values to her children and her vassals. Her court became a haven for artists and poets across Europe. A favourite topic was the legend of King Arthur, Lancelot and Guinevere. Fair Guinevere, King Arthur's queen, supposedly looked like Queen Eleanor. Yet to me

Guinevere seems a pale shadow of the charming, daring, intelligent and independent Eleanor of Aquitaine. The nuns in the convent where she died said of Queen Eleanor that 'She enhanced the grandeur of her birth by the honesty of her life ... She surpassed almost all the queens of the world.'

 FRANCE

ELEANOR'S POSSESSIONS

HENRY'S POSSESSIONS

OTHER LANDS OWING ALLEGIANCE TO FRANCE

1. Eleanor was born and married to Louis VII in Bordeaux.

2. Paris was dull, conservative and disapproving of Eleanor.

3. On her way home from the Crusades, Eleanor was lost at sea for two months.

4. After marrying Henry II, Eleanor lived much of her time in London.

5. Henry gave Eleanor's favourite castle at Woodstock to his new lady love. Eleanor was rumoured to have poisoned her.

6. After leaving Henry, Eleanor ruled Aquitaine from Poitiers, her favourite city.

7. Henry imprisoned Eleanor in a castle at Salisbury for sixteen years.

8. After the Third Crusade, Eleanor and her son Richard visited Nottingham and Sherwood Forest. Prince John's support had come from there, as did tales about the loyal Robin Hood.

9. Eleanor died in the Abbey at Fonterraud, where she and Richard the Lion Heart are both buried. Their tombs and statues are still there.

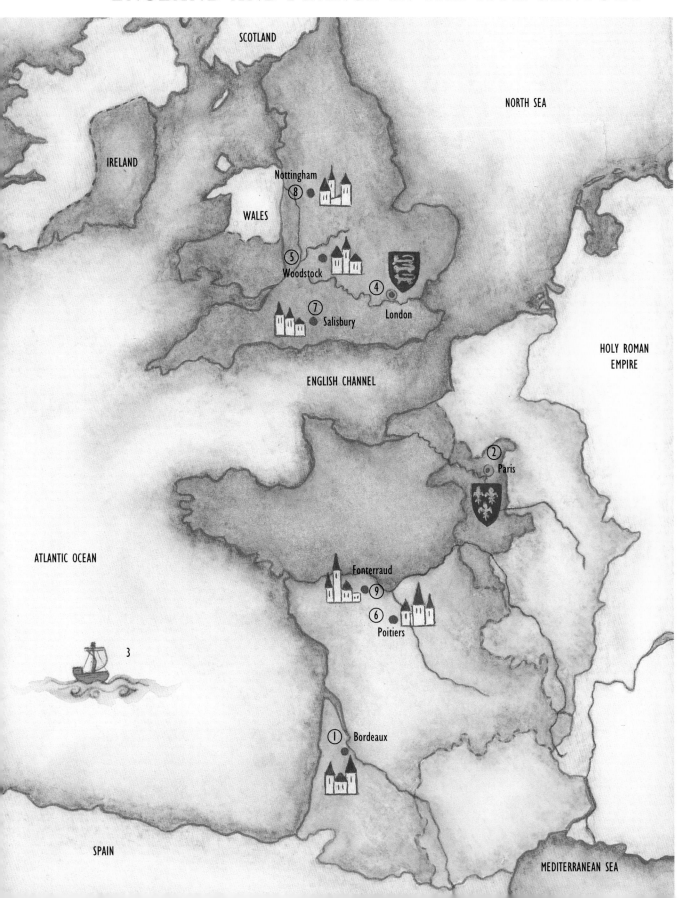

ENGLAND AND FRANCE IN THE 12TH CENTURY

SCOTLAND

NORTH SEA

IRELAND

Nottingham
⑧

WALES

⑤
Woodstock

④
London

⑦ Salisbury

HOLY ROMAN
EMPIRE

ENGLISH CHANNEL

② Paris

ATLANTIC OCEAN

Fonterraud
⑨

⑥
Poitiers

3

① Bordeaux

SPAIN

MEDITERRANEAN SEA

Joan *of* Arc

In 1428, France and England had been at war for a hundred years. Feudalism collapsed while rival kings tore France apart. The French people were impoverished and war weary. English and French soldier-brigands roamed the countryside, attacking villages, stealing and killing.

That year, a teenage girl sought out Dauphin (Prince) Charles, the French claimant to the throne. He was in disguise, but she strode straight up to him and bowed. Announcing to his followers that she was sent by God to save France from the English, she said she must free the besieged city of Orleans, then lead Charles to the city of Reims to be crowned. She promised that the English would be driven out. The girl then spoke with Charles privately. No one knows what she said, but her secret message convinced him to trust her. Many of Charles' courtiers were jealous of Joan.

Soon, outfitted as a knight, Joan led Charles' army against the English. She had a special sword, found behind a church altar – right where she said it would be – and a banner. The French people rallied to her cause, and soon Orleans was free and Charles was crowned at Reims (where all kings of France had to be crowned), deep in enemy territory. The English, suddenly losing the war, hated and feared her, calling her a harlot in men's clothes, and a witch, because a mere girl couldn't lead a victorious army.

Joan of Arc, as we call her today, had experiences that we don't understand. Born around 1412, from the age of thirteen this peasant girl had heard comforting voices of saints and angels. They called her to a great destiny: to save France. Joan had resisted her mission as long as she could, certain she couldn't do it. Finally, she submitted.

In one year, Joan accomplished the tasks set by her voices – led by Joan the French army broke the English siege of Orleans, and achieved other victories on the way to Reims. With Charles crowned, Joan then wanted to pursue the English. But jealous advisors opposed her advice, and King Charles hesitated.

Joan's voices warned that the English would capture her soon. In one battle, they did. After imprisoning and abusing her for months, they tried her for witchcraft and heresy. Standing up to her accusers, she defended herself bravely and intelligently. Convicted of heresy, Joan was condemned and burned at the stake at Rouen in 1431. Witnesses, most of them her enemies, were deeply shaken by the experience. One cried out, 'We are lost, we have burned a saint.' Joan was only nineteen years old.

FAITH, HERESY AND SUPERSTITION

Joan of Arc was canonised in 1920, becoming a saint in the Catholic church. Surrounded by legend, she is also honoured by the French as a national heroine. But for twenty years after her capture and death, Charles and his advisors seemed to forget her. Finally, when her predictions had come true – the English were defeated and Charles secure – he called together a new church court. It declared Joan innocent of the charges against her. Those charges had accused her of witchcraft and disobedience to the Catholic church, or heresy. The English hadn't just hated Joan because she was a symbol of hope to the French – they truly believed she was a witch. In those days, superstition had as much power over people's minds as religion.

The French Dauphin Charles was astounded when Joan knew him from his courtiers.

Any unusual behaviour was considered suspicious, and Joan had done many things to arouse people's fears. She could predict future events, she wore men's clothing, and above all, she heard voices. When she refused to admit that her voices were false, she became a heretic in English eyes. Joan, by following her own conscience, had set herself above Church authority. Ironically, French churchmen had examined her and declared her voices to be true.

Joan defended herself alone and ably against the charges made, but the outcome was never in doubt.

One of two rival Popes lived in Avignon. The French followed him, while the English followed the other Pope in Rome. Joan was tossed about by forces beyond her control. She stayed true to her voices while kings, nobles, and clergy battled around her. Her heroism was not only on the battlefield, but in the courtroom and at the stake.

WHO WAS THE REAL JOAN OF ARC?

One of the most famous heroines in history, Joan of Arc still touches us today. She turned the tide of the Hundred Years' War. She helped ordinary French people decide what they wanted, and raised their morale in fighting the English. As time passed, the French people turned her into a symbol of faith and resistance.

Her name, Jehanne Tarc, was changed to Jeanne d'Arc because d'Arc ('of Arc' in French) sounded more noble to them.

Many strange stories have grown up around Joan over the centuries. One says that she was really leader of a European witch conspiracy, and planned to overthrow Christianity.

Another story claims that she was actually King Charles' half-sister, secretly raised by the Tarcs. Her private meeting with him convinced him of this, which is why he believed in her. In one version of this story Joan was secretly saved and spirited away by Charles' men, while another real witch was burned instead.

In fact, several women claiming to be Joan came forward soon after her death. One even got Joan's brothers to go along with her, trying to benefit from Joan's fame. Then she was discredited and disappeared.

We will never know much about the real Joan. Was she a genius, a superstitious peasant, or a saint? Joan lived such a short time, changed history, and then died a terrible death.

JOAN'S BATTLE SITES

ENGLAND'S POSSESSIONS IN FRANCE

LOYAL TO CHARLES

VASSALS OF FRANCE ALLIED TO ENGLAND

The cannons show the sites of battles Joan took part in.

1. Joan was born in the village of Domremy. It was attacked by brigands when she was little.
2. Joan made the long journey to Dauphin Charles' castle in Chinon, disguised as a man.
3. In Poitiers Joan was examined by Church authorities, who decided her visions were from God, not Satan.
4. Avignon was the home of the Popes in the 14th century. At one point, rival Popes lived in Avignon and Rome. Their rivalry divided the English and French clergy, until the 'Great Schism' ended in 1417. The clergy was still affected by the Schism and by the politics of their own countries.
5. Joan led the Dauphin deep into enemy territory to have him crowned in Reims cathedral.
6. Joan was captured in a skirmish near Compiegne.
7. Joan was ransomed to the English, who tried and burned her to death in Rouen.

FRANCE IN 1427

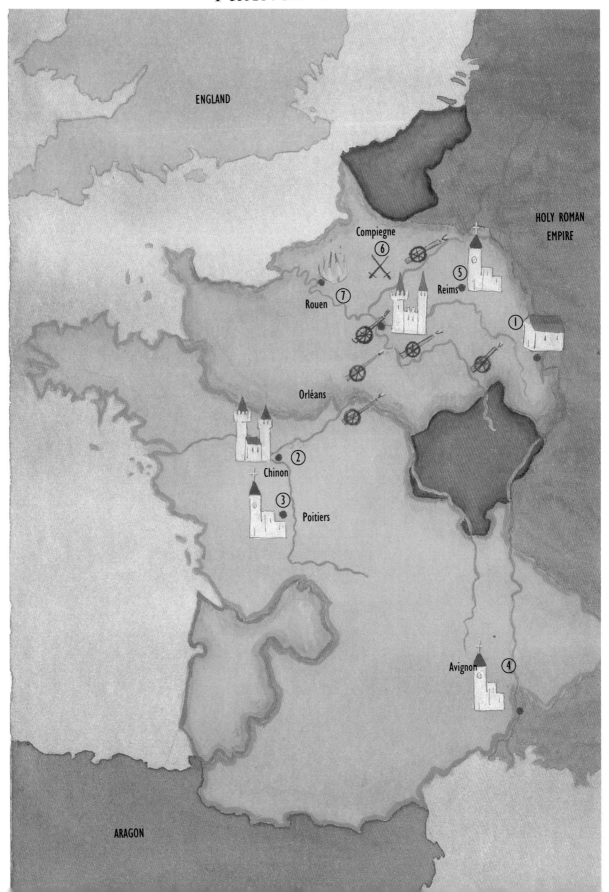

ENGLAND

HOLY ROMAN
EMPIRE

Compiegne
⑥

⑤
Reims

Rouen
⑦

①

Orléans

②

Chinon

③
Poitiers

Avignon ④

ARAGON

Queen Elizabeth I

In 1558, Elizabeth I became Queen of an England torn by strife and threatened by France and Spain. During her reign she stabilised her country, gave it a sense of identity, made it into a great sea power, and allowed the arts to flourish. 'Good Queen Bess' became one of the greatest monarchs in English history, and her greatness came as much from her weaknesses as from her strengths.

Elizabeth grew up surrounded by danger. Her father, Henry VIII, had her mother, Anne Boleyn, executed. Competing political groups hatched plots around her. She knew she could be arrested – even executed – at any time. When her older half-sister Mary became queen she imprisoned Elizabeth briefly. Princess Elizabeth learned early to give 'answers answerless' that kept her safe.

As queen, she needed 'answers answerless' to bring peace to England. Since Henry VIII had founded a Protestant state church, Catholics and Protestants had learned to hate each other. Catholic Mary had persecuted Protestants. Now Protestants hoped Queen Elizabeth would persecute Catholics. Instead she worked hard to keep everyone happy.

One royal suitor after another courted her, but she had no desire to share her throne and lose her power to a husband. By not marrying, she remained on friendly but neutral terms with other monarchs, and always kept them guessing.

Elizabeth's elusive style didn't always work. Her own cousin, Mary Queen of Scots, conspired to overthrow her. Mary, a Catholic, was living in England after fleeing rebellion in her own country, and hoped to become Queen of England herself. After several years of tolerance, Elizabeth reluctantly had Mary executed in 1587.

Claiming to avenge Mary's death, Catholic Spain attacked England with its mighty Armada of ships. Dressed in armour, Elizabeth rallied her people to defend England. Her new modern navy defeated the Armada, establishing England as a great sea power.

Queen Elizabeth ruled for forty-five years. In her later years she was able to encourage the arts and peaceful trade. England became a true nation under her leadership.

THE ELIZABETHAN AGE

In Elizabeth's time, women were thought unfit to reign. She proved this prejudice wrong, however. Unlike many rulers of her day, she spoke and wrote several foreign languages. She dealt directly with envoys and rulers from other countries, playing her own subtle politics. England prospered, not least because its queen avoided expensive wars and controlled national spending.

Queen Elizabeth graciously accepts homage from a peasant girl.

while her nobles await their turn to entertain her.

Elizabeth built the most modern navy of her time, and supported voyages of exploration. Her navy proved itself when it defeated the huge Spanish Armada. Her explorers became famous raiders and traders. Privateers like Sir Francis Drake made daring raids against Spanish ports and treasure ships, bringing back riches to England. Drake also sailed around the world, the first European captain to explore the western American coast.

Queen Elizabeth sponsored exploration in what is now Canada, in hopes of finding a northwest passage to the riches of China. She granted a charter to the East India Company, opening up trade with India. Both Canada and India eventually became part of a vast British Empire.

Elizabeth inspired achievements in literature and drama. She and her court supported people like the poet Edmund Spenser and the dramatist William Shakespeare. In his popular plays, Shakespeare created a powerful national language and gave his countrymen a sense of pride. Elizabeth I was one of his fans.

Having inherited a country torn by religious strife and close to bankruptcy, by the end of the Elizabethan Age Elizabeth had created a united and powerful England, well on its way to becoming a world power.

In sea-outfit (including chest armour), Sir Francis Drake poses in front of a globe given to him by his Queen for circling the earth. A coconut he brought her fits inside it.

THE VIRGIN QUEEN

Queen Elizabeth even used her weaknesses to advantage. She hated making important decisions, to the despair of her advisers. From refusing to execute her cousin Mary Queen of Scots, to ignoring laws against Catholics, she let events unfold and avoided making mistakes.

Her father's six marriages turned Elizabeth against marriage. In any case, any husband – foreign or English – would have tried to dominate her and England. Instead she used courtship as part of her foreign policy.

Queen Elizabeth's marriage was to England. She loved her subjects and worked for their welfare. She and her court regularly travelled around the country to see her people. In turn, they loved her. Children brought her flowers, and she graciously listened to endless speeches by local dignitaries. She dressed gorgeously, to impress people. With her elegant looks, fair skin and red-gold hair, she must have been unforgettable. But she also penny-pinched where she could, making her nobles host her when she travelled. Yet she sold her own jewellery and lands to help England.

Elizabeth I withstood repeated threats to her kingdom and to her life. But by not marrying and having children, the Virgin Queen had no one to succeed her. She refused to name an heir to her throne until she was dying, because she feared plots to dethrone her.

Towards the end of her life, she made a speech. In it she said, 'I do assure you there is no prince that loveth his subjects better ... There is no jewel, be it of never so rich a price, which I set before this jewel: I mean your love.' In Eleanor of Aquitaine's time, no monarch would have made such a claim. For Queen Elizabeth, her people came first.

1. Queen Elizabeth was born in London, and lived most of her life there.
2. Queen Elizabeth sponsored ship building and voyages of exploration around the world.
3. Kept in seclusion in different locations, Mary Queen of Scots never stopped plotting against Queen Elizabeth. The two queens never met. Rulers and nobles from many countries sought marriage with Queen Elizabeth, including:
4. King Philip II of Spain, Queen Elizabeth's widowed former brother-in-law.
5. The Earl of Arran in Scotland.
6. Crown Prince Eric, later King of Sweden.
7. King Charles IX of France, his younger brother Duke Henry of Anjou (later King Henry III of France and King of Poland) and Francois, Duke of Alencon.
8. Duke Emmanuel Philibert of Savoy.
9. Archduke Charles of the Holy Roman Empire.
10. Archduke Ferdinand of the Holy Roman Empire.
11. The Spanish Armada met its doom attempting to invade England. The English fleet and a sudden storm were too much for the huge ships.
12. After Queen Elizabeth's death, Mary Queen of Scots' son James became King.

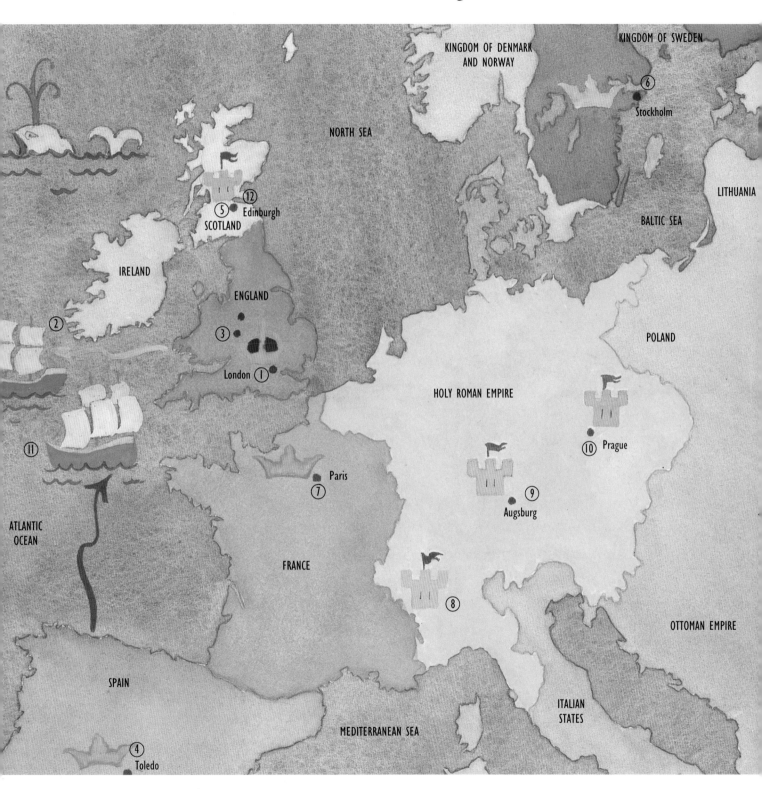

KINGDOM OF DENMARK
AND NORWAY

KINGDOM OF SWEDEN

⑥
Stockholm

NORTH SEA

LITHUANIA

BALTIC SEA

⑫
⑤ Edinburgh
SCOTLAND

IRELAND

ENGLAND

POLAND

②

③

London ①

HOLY ROMAN EMPIRE

⑩ Prague

Paris
⑦

⑪

⑨
Augsburg

ATLANTIC
OCEAN

FRANCE

⑧

OTTOMAN EMPIRE

SPAIN

MEDITERRANEAN SEA

ITALIAN
STATES

④
Toledo

Sacajawea

Two hundred years ago, the prairies of North America were the territories of many different tribes. There they lived, hunted game, traded and sometimes fought each other. Around 1794, enemy hunters captured a Shoshoni girl in a raid. She grew up far from her people, a slave among foreign masters. Though she learned their ways, she still dreamed of returning to her family. Her name was Sacajawea.

When she was about seventeen, a French-Canadian fur trader called Toussaint Charbonneau acquired Sacajawea as one of his slave-wives. Soon after, Merriweather Lewis and William Clark hired him as a guide. These great American explorers and their men were seeking an overland passage to the Pacific Ocean. The trader insisted that Sacajawea come with him.

With her two-month-old son strapped to her back, young Sacajawea set off with the expedition in 1805. Without her, it would have failed. From cooking, cleaning and finding edible plants to showing them important passageways through the wilderness, Sacajawea was indispensable. Once when a boat capsized she saved the expedition records. Using spoken and sign language, she reassured the tribes they met that the expedition was peaceful. Though Sacajawea grew increasingly ill, she stayed cheerful, unselfish and patient. All the while, she cared for her baby.

Late in their journey, the exhausted group met a band of suspicious natives. Suddenly, Sacajawea threw her arms around the chief, weeping and laughing. In all that vast wilderness, she had found her brother! He gave the expedition horses and a guide, enabling it to reach the Pacific Ocean. Sacajawea continued with them, returning to Missouri. It must have been hard to leave her tribe behind again.

Although she never received payment for her services, Sacajawea became one of the most celebrated women in the history of the United States. A river, a mountain peak and a mountain pass in Montana are named after her. Statues and monuments stand in Oregon, Montana and Idaho to honour her.

No one knows for certain what became of Sacajawea. Three different states claim her grave site. Some historians say she died of a fever when she was only twenty-five. The version I like to believe is that she escaped from her husband and slowly made her way back to her own people, where she became a respected elder. She may have died in 1884 when she was almost 100 years old, home again at last.

A TIME OF GREAT CHANGE IN AMERICA

Thousands of years ago, nomadic peoples crossed from Asia to the Americas. Hunting on foot and fishing in boats, they travelled along a land bridge that stretched from Alaska to Russia during the Ice Age. They didn't know they had entered a new continent.

As they spread all across the Americas, these peoples learned to live in many different surroundings. Change came gradually, when one group moved to a new area, or traders brought new ideas.

When Europeans came to the Americas, they altered the balance of life there. By the time Lewis and Clark met Sacajawea, the lives of Native Americans had been changed by disease, horses and guns.

Eagles were sacred to natives across North America, and the bald eagle was adopted as the national bird of the USA.

Many natives were hit by diseases from Europe like measles, chicken pox and small-pox. Deadly plagues swept North and South America because native people had no immunity. By the end of the nineteenth century, up to nine out of every ten native people may have died. Between the times of Joan of Arc and Elizabeth I, a plague called the Black Death had devastated Europe, but this was unimagin-ably worse. Epidemics struck again and again, right through the nineteenth century. The Lewis and Clark expedition passed villages emptied by plague, and Sacajawea's captors were later wiped out by smallpox.

Horses changed life for many native tribes. Across central North America, huge herds of bison roamed its Great Plains. Natives hunted them and other animals to use for food, clothing, and tools. When they got horses from European explorers, they could travel farther and hunt bison and other game more easily. Sacajawea came from the Great Plains area, and her tribe was famous for its fine horses.

Along with horses, natives got guns from white people. A gun could kill more game. It could also kill more people. With guns and horses came more competition for game animals, more serious warfare among tribes, and more death.

White people didn't understand Native Americans or how they had changed their lives.

Sacajawea witnessed the end of a magical time, when bison were plentiful and native Americans were free to follow their own ways.

They saw natives not as people but as 'noble savages' or as 'heathens', to be conquered. Between the time of Columbus and the time of Lewis and Clark – only 300 years – the world of Native Americans had changed dramatically. In another 100 years, their many nations would be invaded and forced onto reservations. Not understanding that each tribe belonged to its surroundings, white people would often force them to live far from the lands they knew and loved.

SACAJAWEA'S WORLD

Sacajawea's small Shoshoni tribe lived on the western edge of the Plains, among dry mountains and hills. They were nomads, skilful at finding wild plants and animals in a barren land. They competed for bison with strong hunter-warrior tribes, like Blackfoot and Crow, to their east.

Further east were the Hidatsa and Mandans, who lived in earth lodge villages along the Missouri River. The men hunted bison on the Plains, while the women farmed. Their villages were centres for trade among natives and whites. Sacajawea grew up there as a slave after Hidatsa hunters captured her. While some children were adopted and became members of their new tribe, Sacajawea evidently was traded and sold repeatedly.

Different tribes had their own traditions, but they shared much with other tribes. The Crow and Hidatsa, for example, spoke the same language. The Plains tribes also shared a sign language that worked as well as words. Sacajawea learned new skills and languages from her masters, which she used to help Lewis and Clark.

Although they expressed it in different ways, these tribes also thought of plants and animals as their relatives. The land and its creatures were full of power that a person could tap in to for guidance and inspiration. Dreams, visions, rituals and ceremonies all expressed this sense of sacred power. Sacajawea must have gained strength and courage from this outlook.

With so many skills, perhaps Sacajawea could have escaped her husband, made her way back to her tribe, and lived to be a wise old woman. We will never know, any more than Sacajawea knew that she was making history.

SACAJAWEA'S WORLD, AROUND 1805

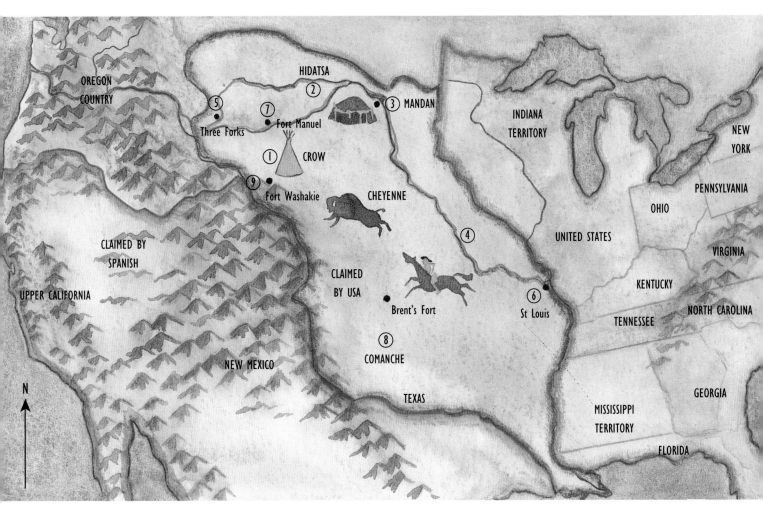

1. Sacajawea was born a Shoshoni.

2. Sacajawea was captured and raised by Hidatsas.

3. Sacajawea was later sold to Mandans, who sold her to Toussaint Charbonneau, future guide to the Lewis and Clark expedition.

4. The route of the Lewis and Clark expedition. They followed the Missouri River, then journeyed through Oregon Country, reached the Pacific Ocean and returned, following another branch of the Missouri River on the way home. Lewis and Clark were exploring part of the land claims 'bought' from France in the Louisiana purchase.

5. Sacajawea was reunited briefly with her brother, but had to continue with the expedition.

6. The Charbonneaus settled in St Louis.

7. Did Sacajawea die here?

8. Or did she escape from her husband, flee south through Brent's Fort to live with the Comanche, a southern branch of the Shoshoni, re-marry, have children and die there?

9. Or did Sacajawea return home and die on the Shoshoni reservation in Wyoming?

Harriet Tubman

An escaped slave from a Maryland plantation, Harriet Tubman was called 'the Moses of her people' by her fellow slaves. Before the American Civil War, she led other slaves to freedom. During the war, she worked for the Union as a nurse and spy, and afterwards, she campaigned for Black education and women's rights.

Harriet Tubman was born around 1821. Named Araminta Ross, she grew up a rebellious slave, often whipped for disobedience. She also belonged to a loving family. When two of her sisters were sold, she began having nightmares about being sold too. When she grew up she called herself Harriet, after her mother.

When she was about fifteen, Harriet stepped between her owner and a runaway slave. The owner hurled a two-pound weight at the fleeing man. It hit Harriet in her forehead, denting her skull into her brain and nearly killing her. She took months to recover. Afterwards the pressure on her brain made her sometimes stagger or suddenly fall asleep.

Harriet became deeply religious, and began having dreams that foretold future events. They called her to escape. Meanwhile, she pretended to be stupid and slow so no one would buy her.

She married a free man, John Tubman, in 1844 or 1845, but in 1849 Harriet found out she was to be sold. Her husband didn't want to run away, so she escaped to Pennsylvania alone.

For Harriet, her own freedom was not enough – she felt called to free others. Within a year, she came back for her own family and as many other slaves as wanted to go with her. She returned to Maryland nineteen times over the next decade, bringing out all her remaining family, and over 100 others.

In 1850, the Fugitive Slave Law passed Congress, allowing slave owners to track runaways into free states. With the help of the Underground Railroad, a network of those who helped escaped slaves, Harriet Tubman took people all the way to Canada. She became famous with abolitionists – people who opposed slavery and campaigned to stop it.

With the outbreak of the Civil War, Harriet Tubman used her connections to get work with the Union Army in South Carolina. She did nursing, taught freed slaves job skills and ran spy missions. 'General' Tubman remains the only woman in US history to plan and lead a military campaign, in a raid that freed 750 slaves.

After the war, she raised money for Black education and women's right to vote. Harriet supported family and friends by nursing, cooking, housekeeping and raising chickens and vegetables to sell. Harriet Tubman died in 1913, still suffering from the sleeping spells that had never stopped her from freeing others.

SLAVERY IN THE UNITED STATES

Starting in the sixteenth century, thousands of Africans were kidnapped and shipped to the Americas. Those who survived the horrors of the voyage were sold as slaves. Regarded as less than human, most were housed in primitive shacks, fed poorly, and abused by their owners.

Across the southern United States, slaves laboured in cotton, rice and sugar plantations. The work was brutal, and replacements were constantly needed. Some plantation owners, like Harriet Tubman's owner, actually bred slaves to sell, especially after 1807, when importing slaves was outlawed. By the early 1800s there were over 1 ½ million slaves living in the United States.

By the mid-1800s, the cruelty of this 'peculiar institution' had outraged many people. Canada and the northern United States had already outlawed it. However, even slave owners who disapproved of slavery in principle weren't ready to give it up: their wealth depended on it.

Meanwhile, slaves ran away, often with help from sympathetic white people. The penalties for helping an escaped slave were severe, and a captured slave could be beaten, mutilated and sold into worse working conditions. Yet up to 100,000 people escaped over the years rather than endure slavery.

Though others helped more slaves escape than she did, Harriet Tubman was the Underground Railroad's most successful conductor. The name Moses helped her, because slave owners thought 'Moses' was a man and weren't looking for a woman. Harriet's fame inspired many other slaves to escape.

Two views of slavery: owners put up 'Wanted' posters showing a healthy, well-dressed runaway. Abolitionists showed a helpless victim.

'OLE CHARIOT'

Imagine running for your life, frightened and hungry. The woman guiding you takes you through swamps and thick woods you've never seen before. You all pause to rest and suddenly your guide falls asleep. You wait patiently to go on, because you trust her totally. She is 'Moses'.

Harriet Tubman never learned to read or write, but she always outsmarted slave owners. She developed an escape system, starting out with her group on a Saturday night. Since Sunday wasn't a work day, the runaways might not be missed until Monday. Once their owners knew their slaves were missing, they posted notices describing the runaways. Harriet hired people to take the notices down.

Sometimes Harriet dressed as a man, or imitated an old woman hobbling down the road, while she spied out the land. She then used code songs to let her people know when to stay hidden and when they were safe. Based on 'spirituals', they were full of double meanings. She herself became the 'Ole Chariot' who carried slaves to freedom across the Jordan (the boundary between North and South).

When she could, Harriet Tubman taught freed slaves job skills so they could take their place in society. She opened a laundry for the Union Army in South Carolina, run by ex-slaves.

As 'General' Tubman, Harriet carried a gun with her to rally the faint-hearted. 'Go north or die,' she would threaten anyone who wanted to turn back - and she meant it.

During the Civil War, Harriet used her skills as a spy, helping even more slaves escape to freedom. During and after the war, she worked as a nurse, using home remedies to help wounded soldiers, and gaining a reputation as a miracle worker.

Harriet Tubman's efforts went unrewarded for most of her life. Only in 1898, when she was seventy-eight years old, did she receive a $20 a month pension from Congress. She was never paid for her work as a nurse and spy. Yet she had so many friends, some famous and powerful like the writer and philosopher Ralph Waldo Emerson, that she could count on help whenever she needed it. She even received a shawl and a medal from Queen Victoria of England. The Queen invited her to her birthday party in 1897, but Harriet declined with thanks.

USA AND SLAVERY IN THE MID-19TH CENTURY

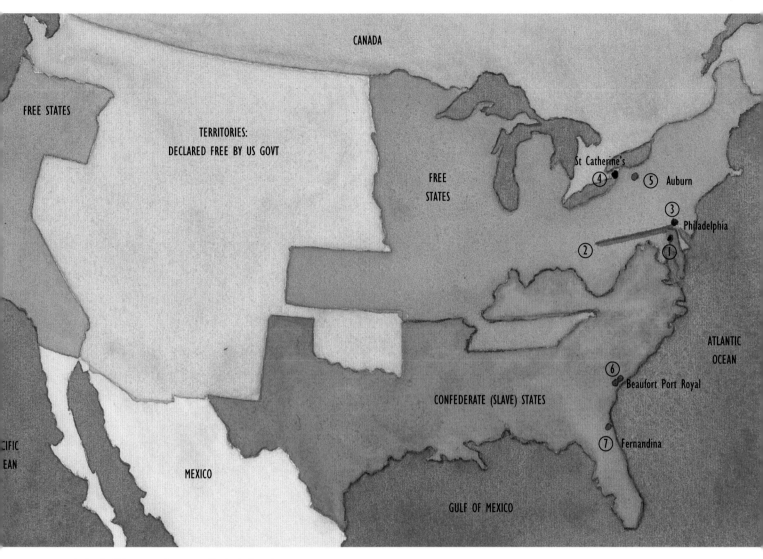

1. Harriet Tubman was born on a Maryland plantation.

2. To gain freedom, she had to cross the Mason and Dixon Line, the boundary between Pennsylvania and Maryland, and unofficial boundary between freedom and slavery.

3. Harriet escaped to Philadelphia, Pennsylvania. From there she returned to Maryland to rescue other slaves.

4. After the Fugitive Slave Law was passed, Harriet led her escapees to St Catherine's, Canada.

5. Her friend William Seward helped Harriet buy a home. He later became US Vice President under Abraham Lincoln.

6. During the Civil War, Harriet worked in two South Carolina army posts as nurse, spy and liaison with ex-slaves.

7. Harriet was sent to work as a nurse in Florida.

Marie Curie

For Marya (later Marie) Sklodowska Curie, scientific discovery was an adventure. The first great woman scientist in history, she did research on the nature of radioactivity, received two Nobel prizes, and promoted x-ray and radiation therapy.

Born in Russian-dominated Poland in 1867, Marie Sklodowska grew up valuing knowledge and service to society. Although desperately poor, she studied mathematics and chemistry at the great Sorbonne University in Paris, France, where she met scientist Pierre Curie. They married in 1895 and embarked together on an adventure of scientific discovery. He was older and well-established, but they worked as complete equals. They published all their findings together, so it could not be said one had done more than the other.

The Curies were fascinated by what Marie named 'radioactivity'. They discovered two new radioactive elements, the first one of which Marie called polonium, for her beloved Poland. The second one took years to isolate. Working in an old shed, Marie single-handedly processed tons of pitchblende ore to produce one gram of a new, extremely radioactive element: radium. Radium soon proved useful in treating cancer, and radiation treatment is still used today. Rather than profit by their discovery, the Curies gave Marie's process for extracting radium to the world. Their work won them the coveted Nobel Prize in 1903, and made them famous.

In 1906 Pierre was killed in a traffic accident. Marie was devastated. Alone, with two young daughters to raise, she decided to continue her research on radioactivity, to publish and to teach. She knew her husband would not have wanted her to stop. Marie received a second Nobel Prize in 1911, which she dedicated to her husband's memory.

During the First World War, Marie realised that newly-invented x-ray machines could save thousands of lives. She taught herself to operate the machines and to drive. Having outfitted over 200 donated cars she and other volunteers brought them to battlefield hospitals. Over a million wounded soldiers were x-rayed for bullets and shrapnel. Knowing exactly where to operate, doctors were able to save countless lives.

Exposed to radiation for years, Marie Curie died from radiation poisoning in 1934. Her pioneering efforts are still leading to new discoveries. She was a rare and stubborn genius, dedicated both to learning and to benefiting others, willing to make sacrifices most of us would find overwhelming.

fluorine 10 Ne neon 11 Na sodium 12 Mg magnesium 13 Al aluminium 14 Si silicon 15 P phosphorus 6 S sulphur 17 Cl chlorine 18 Ar argon 19 K potassium 20 Ca calcium 21 Sc scandium 22 Ti titanium 23 vanadium 24 Cr chromium 25 Mn manganese 26 Fe iron 27 Co cobalt 28 Ni nickel 29 Cu copper 30 Zn

inc 31 Ga gal ... 37 Rb rubid-
um 38 Sr str ... Tc Tc tech-
etium 44 Ru ... n indium 50
n tin 51 Sb ... arium 57 La
nthanum 58 ... samarium 63
u europium ... bium 69 Tm
hulium 70 Yl ... Re rhenium
6 Os osmium ... b lead 83 Bi
ismuth 84 P ... inium 90 Th
horium 91 Pa ... icium 96 Cm
urium 97 Bk ... endelevium
02 No nobeli ... 5 B boron 6
carbon 7 N ... esium 13 Al
luminium 14 ... ssium 20 Ca
alcium 21 Sc ... 6 Fe iron 27
o cobalt 28 ... enic 34 sele-
ium 35 Br b ... irconium 41
b niobium 4 ... d palladium
7 AG silver 4 ... odine 54 Xe
enon 55 Cs ca ... neodymium
I Pm prome ... Dy dyspro-
ium 67 Ho h ... fnium 73 Ta
antalum 74 V ... gold 80 Hg
ercury 81 T ... radon 87 Fr
ancium 88 R ... neptunium
4 Pu plutoni ... einsteinium
00 Fm fermi ... n I H hydro-
en 2 He heliu ... 9 F fluorine
0 Ne neon 11 ... 16 S sulphur

7 Cl chlorine 18 Ar argon 19 K potassium 20 Ca calcium 21 Sc scandium 22 Ti titanium 23 V vanadium 4 Cr chromium 25 Mn manganese 26 Fe iron 27 Co cobalt 28 Ni nickel 29 Cu copper 30 Zn zinc 31 Ga allium 32 Ge germanium 33 As arsenic 34 selenium 35 Br bromine 36 Kr krypton 37 Rb rubidium 38 Sr trontium 39 Y yttrium 40 Zr zirconium 41 Nb niobium 42 Mo molybdenum 43 Tc Tc technetium 44 Ru

SCIENTIFIC PIONEERS

In ancient times, the basic elements were thought to be air, fire, earth and water. By Marie Curie's day, scientists had realised that there are many elements. However, atomic elements were supposed to be stable and unchanging. The Curies' research showed that certain extremely heavy elements existed. These were very slowly breaking down into lighter elements by shooting off bits of themselves. Marie named this process radioactivity.

Like the great Albert Einstein's theories of relativity, the Curies' discoveries led to a new way of seeing the physical world. From the smallest particle to the vast universe, things were no longer solid and predictable. Scientists had to discover new principles to understand and describe how the world worked. With these new discoveries, the age of technology in which we live was born.

Marie Curie contributed a special approach to science. She hated seeing countries keep their scientists' work secret, and instead wanted a world where all countries could share and benefit from each other's discoveries.

Neither Marie nor Pierre believed in taking advantage of their discoveries. They could have become millionaires by patenting her method of extracting radium, but the idea of benefiting from her work in that way appalled them. Honours, however, poured in from around the world. By her death, in addition to two

Alchemists were the first chemists: they worked with the four elements trying to turn lead into gold and in doing so discovered new elements.

Nobel Prizes, Marie had received 137 prizes, medals, awards, honorary doctorates, and memberships of important scientific organisations.

What Marie really wanted was a decent laboratory where she and others could work. France built her a research centre in 1914, but war overtook her plans for four years. A second research centre was established in Poland. In these centres, physicists and chemists were able to continue building on the Curies' original discoveries. Marie Curie would have been proud to know that one of those scientists, her daughter Irene, became a Nobel Prize winner in 1935, a year after her mother's death.

A UNIQUE COMMITMENT

Marie Sklodowska's family loved music, books and learning. In addition they believed deeply in serving others, values Marie stayed committed to all her life. She wanted to go to university – difficult for any woman of her time, but especially for one with little money. While a student, she lived so close to starvation that she actually fainted from lack of food. She didn't mind, she was so happy to be doing what she wanted.

Pierre Curie was a perfect companion. He was so interested in his scientific pursuits that he sometimes forgot to eat or sleep. Curious about the newly discovered element of radium, he tried putting some on his arm to see what would happen. It burned a hole in his skin! They made an eccentric but very happy couple, devoted to their work.

Neither of them knew how dangerous radioactive materials were. The notes and journals they used are still radioac-

Pierre and Marie Curie were devoted to each other and to science.

tive today. By the time Marie Curie died, her body was saturated with radioactivity. Ironically, she was killed by the very substance that has healed so many other people. Yet I don't think she minded: Marie was one of the most determined idealists who ever lived.

We can imagine Marie in the middle of a snowy winter, shovelling pitchblende ore into a boiling kettle in her freezing, draughty shed. While it melts down, ready for the next stage of extraction, she waits patiently. After years of such work she isolates one gram of pure radium, a tiny bit of concentrated radioactivity. That night, she enters the dark laboratory where it sits in a jar. It glows, a deep luminous blue. She is supremely happy.

EUROPE BETWEEN 1919 AND 1934

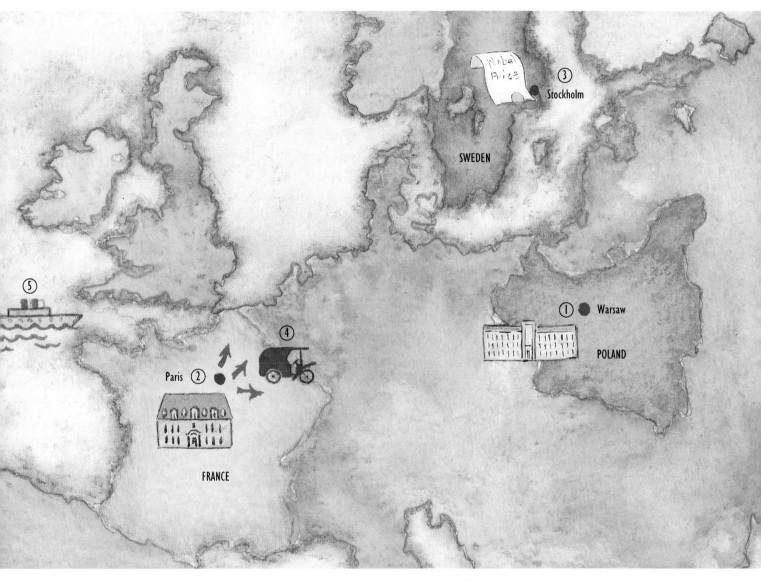

1. Marya Sklodowska was born in Warsaw, Poland, under Russian domination. She was always a Polish patriot. Later, after Poland gained independence from Russia, she built a Radium Institute in Warsaw.

2. 'Marie' Sklodowska had to study in Paris because women were prevented by Russian law from going to university in Poland.

3. Marie and Pierre Curie received the 1903 Nobel Prize in Stockholm. Marie also received the 1911 Nobel Prize.

4. During the First World War, Marie saved many lives by bringing X-ray technology to the battlefields.

5. Marie made many trips abroad, receiving honours and awards.

Anna Akhmatova

Take my child, take my friend, take away
My secret strange talent for song.

Anna Akhmatova was born Anna Gorenko in Russia in 1889. She began writing poetry at the age of eleven, growing up during the last years of the Russian Empire, when royal Tsars ruled absolutely, and police spies were everywhere. As she grew older, like many other educated people Anna wanted a fairer system of government, but she was less interested in politics than in feelings. She wrote love poetry.

When the First World War began in 1914, Anna Akhmatova was already a famous poet. Her poems steadily gained fame even during those terrible times, and during the equally fearful Russian Revolution and Civil War. Throughout a life of danger and sorrow, she wrote poems that reflected her times, becoming Russia's greatest woman poet.

After the Civil War, Russia became part of the Communist USSR. Anna's poetry readings attracted huge audiences, but she got into trouble. Communist leaders wanted to create a new society, in which they expected writers to promote the better world Communism would build. Yet Anna saw people starving, homeless and afraid. Under the USSR's ruthless dictator Joseph Stalin, millions of people were dying. Instead of praising Communism, she wrote about what she saw and how people really felt.

Anna's poetry was condemned as traitorous, and from 1924 to 1939 it was banned. Her friends and family were arrested and sent to prison camps, or shot. Secretly, however, she helped other victims of Stalin's terrorism.

During the Second World War, Anna was allowed to publish and give readings of her poetry once more. After the War, she fell out of favour with the Communist leaders again – evidently because she was too popular.

After Stalin's death, Anna Akhmatova was eventually allowed to publish and even travel abroad. The Russian people loved her and her poems. When she died in 1966, thousands went to Anna's funeral. People all over the world are now learning about this brave woman and great poet.

POETRY IN A TIME OF DREAD

... No, no foreign wings protected me.
I was with my people, I was ever
Where my people had the ill luck to be.

Since the nineteenth century, poets have influenced Russia deeply. Russians have expected their poets to guide them with daring thought and beautiful language. Even today, poets can be as popular as rock stars, whether they write about society's ills or more personal things like love.

From 1921 to 1991, Russia was the centre of the first Communist state. As Joseph Stalin rose to power in the 1920s, he turned it into a police state, 'purging' it of millions of 'state enemies'. He suspected everyone, from poet to peasant.

Stalin insisted on 'Socialist Realism' for all art and literature, its purpose being to glorify Stalin and the achievements of Communism.

Nothing could be published inside or outside the country without permission. If someone was forbidden to publish in the USSR, they must remain silent. Anyone who published banned writings outside the country was an 'internal émigré', a traitor who could go to prison.

Some writers secretly gave copies of their work to trusted friends who passed them on

One of the safe subjects for artists and writers was Russian fairy tales.

to others, like chain letters. The samizdat, or self-published system, saved the works of many people who died in the purges. Anna Akhmatova helped distribute her friends' work, and had friends memorise some of her own poems, so she could destroy her manuscripts. She kept other poems in a suitcase that she never let out of her sight, just in case she was arrested.

ANNA AKHMATOVA'S PERSONAL WORLD

For some the breeze can freshly blow.
For some the sunlight wanes at ease,
But we, made partners in our dread,
Hear only grating of the keys,
And heavy-booted soldiers' tread.

Imagine being afraid all the time. Police spy on you, your belongings are rifled when you're not home, and your room is bugged. Sometimes you're allowed to work, sometimes you're homeless because you've offended the authorities. Your friends and family have been arrested and sent to prison camps. Worst of all, others have died for made-up crimes. Like many Russians, Anna Akhmatova's life was like this.

After the Revolution in 1917 and the rise of Communism, Anna faced a conflict between the demands of the State and her need to express what was important to her. The first great Russian poets and authors,

Stalin liked his portraits to make him look handsome and kind.

people like Alexander Pushkin, had felt the same thing under the Tsars.

Anna stayed loyal to her personal vision. Defying the demand to write Socialist Realism, she wrote poetry reflecting the actual fate of her people. Her poem 'Requiem' tells about a mother's grief when her son disappears into Stalin's prison camps, based on her son's three times in prison.

Anna Akhmatova was a heroine to the Russian people. I think she had no choice, however: great poetry tells the truth. Stalin and the Soviet Union are gone, but her poetry lives on.

ANNA AKHMATOVA'S RUSSIA

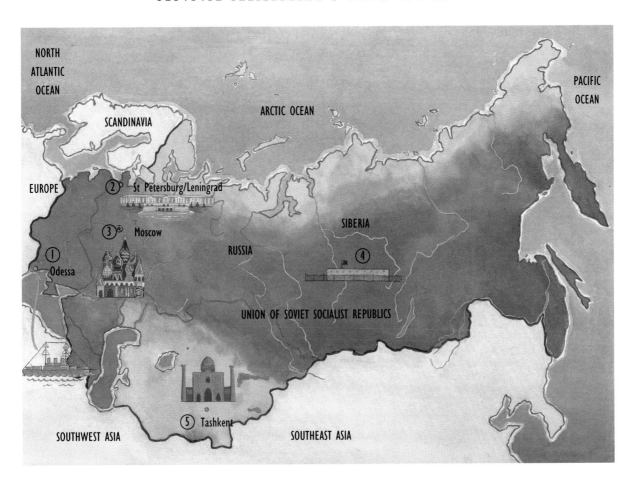

—————————— BOUNDARY OF USSR

—————————— BOUNDARY BETWEEN RUSSIA AND OTHER SOVIET REPUBLICS

1. Odessa, Anna Akhmatova's birthplace. In 1905, sailors mutinied on the battleship Potemkin in its port, as revolution approached.

2. Peter the Great's Summer Palace near Akhmatova's lifetime home of St Petersburg.

3. Akhmatova also lived in Moscow, famous for landmarks like St Basil's Cathedral.

4. Many of Akhmatova's friends disappeared into prison camps in Siberia.

5. During World War II Akhmatova lived in Muslim Tashkent, where mosques like this can be found.

Madame Sun Yat-Sen
(*Soong Ching-ling*)

Madame Sun Yat-Sen was one of the three Soong sisters: her older sister quietly amassed a fortune; her younger sister married a warlord to gain power; but she, Ching-ling, gave up everything for China. Ching-ling was born around 1893 – her name means 'happy outlook'.

The wealthy Soongs educated their children in the USA and worked for revolution at home. Around the time Soong Ching-ling was born in 1893, they began secretly backing Dr Sun Yat-Sen, China's revolutionary hero. Young Soong Ching-ling fell in love with him.

In 1911 China's people overthrew their tyrannical rulers. Dr Sun became the new republic's first President – until greedy warlords pitched the country into civil war. In the midst of this turmoil, he and Soong Ching-ling married in 1914.

For the next ten years Madame Sun helped her husband as he tried to reunite and reform China, in their desperation accepting help from the USSR. In 1925 Dr Sun died, and his grief-stricken widow tried to carry on. Meanwhile, Dr Sun's followers scrambled for power. One ambitious warlord, General Chiang Kai-shek, tried to marry Madame Sun. When he seized the leadership in Dr Sun's name she fled to Europe. Living in poverty, she tried to raise support for an alternative to Communists and warlords, finally returning to China in 1929. Chiang was now its 'Strong Man', aiming for complete power. To her horror the man whom she believed had betrayed her husband's ideals had married her sister.

Madame Sun tried to oppose Chiang publicly, but her prestige as Dr Sun's widow was no match for bullets. General Chiang didn't dare harm her, but his men harassed, arrested or killed anyone else who dared to resist him. Madame Sun was a virtual prisoner. When she spoke out against Chiang, few listened.

Japan invaded China in 1937. Madame Sun energetically raised funds for medical relief and orphanages. After Japan's defeat in the Second World War, civil war erupted again. Madame Sun urged both sides to form a non-Communist, non-warlord government. Instead, in 1949 the Communists won. She chose to stay in China, while Chiang fled.

Though Madame Sun refused to join the Communist Party, it welcomed her advice – she helped write China's new Constitution and became a Vice President of the Republic. She continued working for children's welfare and received several awards before she retired, officially the highest-ranking woman in China.

A COUNTRY IN CRISIS

Since 1644 China had been ruled by the foreign Manchu dynasty. The Manchus came from Manchuria, outside China. Although they adopted Chinese culture, they kept government posts for themselves. The last member of the dynasty was the cruel Empress Dowager, who by poison and cunning had risen from royal concubine to absolute ruler. China's emperor was only a figurehead.

By the time she was dying in 1908, the Empress had allowed foreign countries to dominate China and its economy. England, France, Germany, and the USA bought tea and silk and sold opium, knowing that addicted Chinese would always want more.

Cities like Shanghai became centres for smuggling, drugs, murder and intrigue. General Chiang Kai-shek started his career as a gangster in the Shanghai underworld. After becoming China's strongest warlord he continued to smuggle drugs, even secretly trading with his enemies the Japanese.

Meanwhile, millions of peasants farmed small plots of land allotted by wealthy landlords. Tax collectors demanded taxes for years in advance, so people had to borrow from moneylenders. One flood or dry season could bring disaster.

The cities were no better. Children sold into slavery to factories might be permanently chained in place to a work station. Conditions like these made Communism attractive – it promised revenge as well as prosperity.

After the Chinese Revolution the Suns had hoped to reform China. They wanted to adopt some things from the West, like universal education, modern transportation and new industry and farming methods, and

In 1924, the ailing Dr Sun Yat-Sen and his young wife set off for Peking where he hoped to advise the warlord. He collapsed and died before he got there.

Chiang Kai-shek gained prestige and wealth, and Soong Mei-ling gained power when they married each other. Madame Sun was scandalised to have Chiang for a brother-in-law.

give peasants more land and fairer taxes. They also wanted to break the foreign stranglehold on China and stop the drug traffic.

Dr Sun's reforms had no time to take effect. Support from Western governments could have helped, but instead of backing him they supported the strongest warlord in power.

When warlords took over, only Christian missionaries and the Communists bothered to work with China's millions of peasants. In the end, the Communists won and the West lost a powerful friend.

A WOMAN'S VISION

Madame Sun endured poverty, exile and danger for her country. After her husband's death, she fled to the USSR in time to witness Joseph Stalin turn it into a police state. She moved to Germany and found a country falling into Nazism. Both repelled her.

For associating with the USSR, she was branded a 'Red', meaning a Communist. Communism meant wanting to overthrow governments everywhere, so that all people could work for the common good and no one would exploit anyone else. In reality, Communists could be as ruthless as anyone else, and they were avowed enemies of Western 'Imperialists'. A Red could expect little sympathy from the West.

In Europe, Madame Sun could have accepted money from her family and had an easy life. Instead she returned to China and opposed General Chiang's corrupt government. Though he had the support of Western governments, he did little for his people. He used his marriage to Madame Sun's sister to give himself a positive image.

Madame Sun mistrusted all politicians, including Communists. Still, she refused to leave her beloved China even if she had to cooperate with the Communist government.

In 1966, the government launched a Cultural Revolution, led by students. Until ordered to stop, they harassed Madame Sun as a 'bourgeois reactionary' and ransacked her house. She spent her last years weakened by cancer, though she raised two adopted daughters.

I wonder if she felt her struggles had been worthwhile. Her country was powerful, united, and free from foreign domination and mass drug addiction. People no longer went hungry. Yet China was still a police state.

Madame Sun always insisted that she was a part of the Chinese Revolution, not a member of the Communist Party. When she lay dying, she was inducted into it. Was this an honour? Or was the Party just taking advantage of her name, as her old enemy Chiang had once done?

1. Soong Ching-ling was born in Shanghai and returned there after schooling in the United States.
2. After the 1911 revolution, Dr Sun was elected President, but a warlord seized Peking, China's capital.
3. The Suns were allowed to form a government for another warlord in Canton, until he turned against them. Returning to Peking, Dr Sun collapsed and died.
4. With USSR-trained troops, General Chiang Kai-shek moved north to conquer and unite China. Madame Sun was in Wuhan when he turned against the Communists. With nowhere else to go, she fled overland to the USSR.
5. In Moscow, Madame Sun found herself a virtual prisoner, and a witness to Joseph Stalin's takeover of the USSR.
6. Escaping to Berlin, Germany, Madame Sun tried to raise support for a 'Third Force', neither Communist nor warlord. Fascist Germany and Italy were both friendly with General Chiang's government — until they allied themselves with Japan.
7. After returning to Shanghai, Madame Sun was forced to flee to Hong Kong when Japan invaded China. She went back to Shanghai following the Communist takeover in 1949.
8. Chiang Kai-shek and Madame Sun's family fled to Taiwan. His armies took it over after losing the civil war in China.

▬▬▬▬▬	INDEPENDENT COUNTRIES
▬ ▬ ▬ ▬	SPHERES OF INFLUENCE BY EUROPEAN POWERS
▬▬▬▬▬	BOUNDARIES OF EUROPEAN-DOMINATED EMPIRES
▬▬▬▬▬	BOUNDARIES OF RUSSIAN EMPIRE
▬▬▬▬▬	BOUNDARIES OF SOVIET DOMINATION WHERE DIFFERENT FROM RUSSIAN EMPIRE
▬▬▬▬▬	AREAS INVADED BY JAPAN
▬▬▬▬▬	BOUNDARIES OF CHINESE EMPIRE

IMPERIALISM IN ASIA, 1914-41

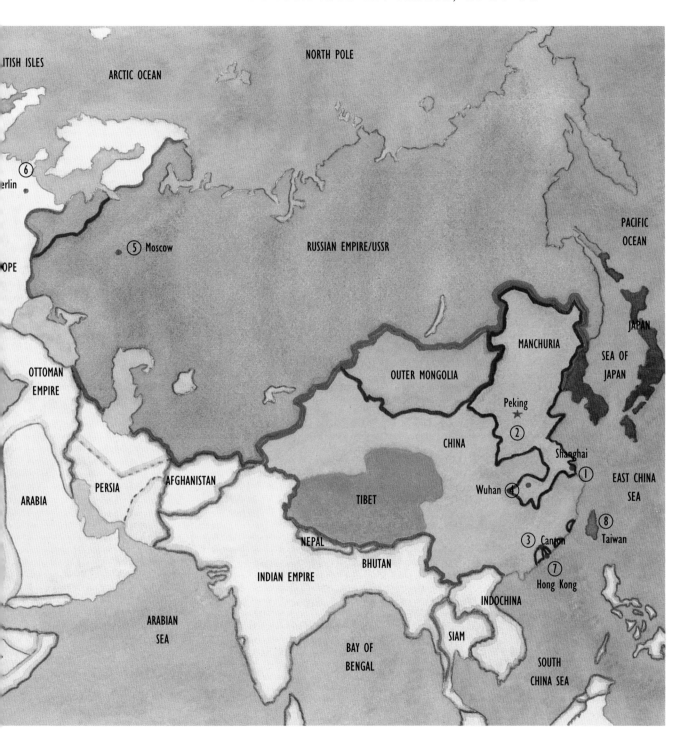

NORTH POLE

ARCTIC OCEAN

ITISH ISLES

⑥
erlin

OPE

PACIFIC
OCEAN

⑤ Moscow

RUSSIAN EMPIRE/USSR

JAPAN

MANCHURIA

SEA OF
JAPAN

OUTER MONGOLIA

OTTOMAN
EMPIRE

Peking
★

CHINA

②

Shanghai

ARABIA

PERSIA

AFGHANISTAN

TIBET

Wuhan ④

①

EAST CHINA
SEA

⑧
Taiwan

NEPAL

③ Canton

INDIAN EMPIRE

BHUTAN

⑦
Hong Kong

INDOCHINA

ARABIAN
SEA

SIAM

BAY OF
BENGAL

SOUTH
CHINA SEA

Amelia Earhart

Amelia Earhart was born in 1897. Even as a little girl she liked adventure. With an unsettled home life, she craved independence but still wanted to help others. She managed to find a career that let her do both.

During the First World War, she visited Canada. Seeing so many soldiers returning wounded, Amelia volunteered as a nurses' aide in a veterans' hospital. She worked ten hours a day until the war ended. Back in the USA, Amelia Earhart took flying lessons, rare for a woman at that time. She was so captivated she even bought her own plane. Although she became a social worker, her passion was flying.

In 1927, Charles Lindbergh made the first solo flight across the Atlantic Ocean. His success fired people's imaginations. A wealthy woman sponsored Amelia Earhart to be the first woman to make the same dangerous flight in 1928, as captain with a crew. Amelia Earhart wrote a book about the trip, which made her famous. Her publisher, George Putnam, also fell in love with her.

Now nicknamed AE, Amelia wanted to fly across the Atlantic by herself someday. Meanwhile, she flew alone across the USA and back again, just for fun. She didn't know it, but this was another first. George Putnam pursued AE until she married him in 1931. He supported her flying adventures, publishing books about them. In 1932, she became the first woman to fly alone across the Atlantic. She set four other world records for solo long distance flights in 1935.

AE also wrote and gave lectures, and did career counselling for young women. Believing that women should have the same opportunities as men, she wanted her success in a 'man's' career to inspire others.

Times changed rapidly. By 1937, planes weren't a novelty, and most records for being 'first to fly' had been set. AE decided to set one more record by flying around the earth at the equator – a difficult trip. Arrangements had to be made in advance all around the world. She and a navigator flew from west to east, all the way across Africa and Asia. AE's flight was big news. US Navy ships would radio her over the wide, empty Pacific Ocean. Then, in a storm over the Pacific, AE's plane disappeared. Although ships combed the ocean looking for a life raft or wreckage, they found neither. The news of her disappearance devastated her fellow Americans: Amelia Earhart was lost forever.

WHAT HAPPENED TO AMELIA EARHART?

Amelia Earhart's mixture of pluck and kindness symbolized what Americans thought of as the best in themselves. For over half a century, they have wondered what happened to their heroine. Her disappearance raised many questions. Did she actually crash in the storm? No trace of the plane was ever found, but the ocean is enormous. Amelia Earhart's last radio messages had seemed way off course. Had her equipment been damaged? Had she planned to spy for the US Navy? Her flight was at night, so what use might it have served?

Did Amelia Earhart spend her last years a prisoner on a Pacific island?

In 1937, the world was preparing for war again. Japan had invaded China, and claimed many Pacific islands. Some of them were off limits to other countries, including the USA, because there were secret military bases on them. Japan never let ships search for Amelia Earhart in its territories. Could she and her navigator have crash-landed on one of Japan's islands and seen military secrets? Spies or not, they would never have been allowed to leave.

After the Second World War, many people investigated Amelia Earhart's disappearance. Despite some evidence that she was captured by the Japanese, both the Japanese and US governments kept silent. As time passed, the chances of solving the mystery faded.

Today, her disappearance seems less important than her accomplishments. She loved flying, and being a woman in a man's world never stopped her. It was her life, not her death, that Amelia would want us to remember.

A LAST FRONTIER

Amelia Earhart saw the possibilities of air flight and promoted it to Americans. Today we take flying for granted, but when Amelia discovered the joy of flying, aeroplanes were not sophisticated. They were not very sturdy, and just getting off the ground was dangerous. A plane would fall apart if it crashed. Every pilot, including AE, took accidents for granted.

Early pilots had a magical bird's eye view of the land below them.

In early planes, people sat in open cockpits, wearing heavy leather jackets, scarves, snug helmets and eye goggles. Once in the air, they never flew very high. Amelia must have loved feeling the wind rush by, and seeing the world spread below her.

There were no charts to guide pilots, or regular airports where they could land. In 1928, Amelia flew across the USA following railroad tracks, roads and rivers shown on maps pinned to her jacket. Once a map blew off and she got lost. Low on fuel, she found a road and followed it to a town, using its main street for a landing strip.

By 1937, planes could fly higher and for longer, and had better equipment. There were flight charts and more airports. Cabins enclosed pilot and passengers: the open cockpit was gone, and the feeling of flying in touch with the elements gone with it. On her last journey, Amelia Earhart had to rely on instruments that told her where she was and how high she was flying. Did she miss the old way of flying? Or was she just happy to be exploring yet one more frontier?

AMELIA EARHART'S WORLD

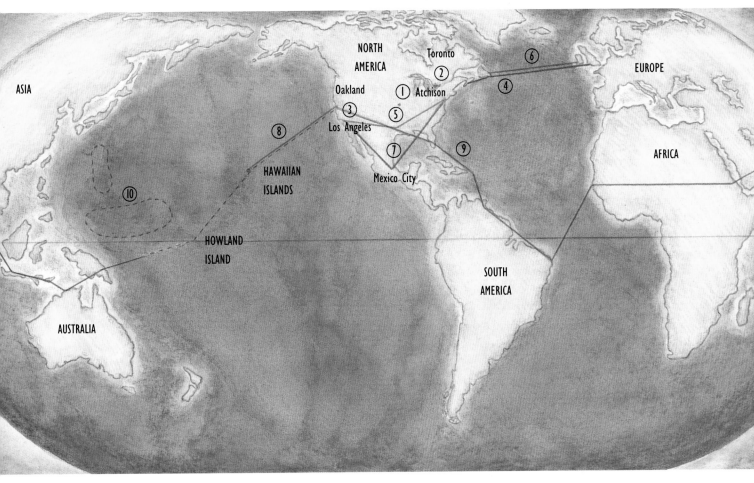

1. Amelia Earhart was born in Atchison, Kansas.

2. She worked in Toronto, Canada, as a volunteer nurse during the First World War.

3. Amelia learned to fly in Los Angeles.

4. As 'captain' of the Friendship, Amelia became the first woman to cross the Atlantic Ocean by plane.

5. Amelia set another 'first' by crossing the US by plane, east to west, then west to east.

6. Determined to justify her fame, Amelia became the first woman to fly solo across the Atlantic Ocean.

7. Amelia was also the first person to fly solo from Los Angeles to Mexico City, and from there to New Jersey.

8. Amelia was the first person to succeed in making the dangerous flight from the mainland US to Hawaii, a much longer flight than the trans-Atlantic crossing.

9. Amelia Earhart's last flight. Broken lines show the part she never completed.

10. Areas controlled by Japan in 1937. Did Amelia stray that far off course?

Frida Kahlo Y Rivera

People don't often think of artists as heroic – art is something to put on a wall, not part of real life. The Mexican artist Frida Kahlo, who was born in 1907, showed how mistaken that thinking is. Her paintings are both personal and universal. They speak of her own feelings, of her pride in being Mexican, and for her whole country.

Although she was cheerful and full of fun, Frida's life was difficult. Childhood polio gave her a limp. In 1925, when she was eighteen, she was severely injured in a bus crash, from which she never fully recovered. She began painting while she was still bedridden, and never stopped. Most of Frida's paintings are self-portraits that express her conflicting emotions. She also used images from Mexico's native and European traditions in her paintings. They seem to ask, 'What does it mean to be Mexican?' and 'Why do I feel pain and joy at the same time?'

Frida married a famous artist, Diego Rivera. Together they travelled abroad, meeting political leaders and other famous artists. Wherever she went, Frida Kahlo wore colourful native clothing, sometimes stopping traffic in foreign cities. She never minded attracting attention. At home, she filled her house with the bright colours, art and furniture of Mexico.

Frida believed in equality for all Mexicans. She and her husband campaigned for education, political rights and social reform to help their people. Many scraped a living on barren land or crowded into the cities looking for work, while rich people ignored or exploited them. Mexicans loved her for championing them at home and abroad.

After thirty-five operations over several years, Frida's health failed. Yet she painted even as she lay dying. When she died in 1954, all Mexico mourned. Her paintings became a national treasure. Frida's home is now a museum where people can see many of her paintings, while others are on view in museums around the world.

FRIDA'S MEXICAN ANCESTRY

Frida Kahlo's ancestors may have descended from several great native civilisations: Olmec, Mayan, Toltec or Aztec. The Aztecs called themselves the Mexica. They ruled much of Mexico from their magnificent island city, Tenochtitlan, where Mexico City now stands. They were great warriors, farmers, artists and astronomers.

The Aztec gods demanded human sacrifice to keep the world in harmony. The Aztec calendar kept track of rituals and sacrifices. It also foretold that in the year Reed One, the exiled white man/god Quetzalcoatl would return from the east to reclaim Mexico and abolish human sacrifice.

In 1519, Reed One by the Aztec calendar, the Spanish adventurer Hernando Cortez arrived in ships from the east. At first, the Aztecs mistook him for Quetzalcoatl and welcomed him. Soon though, Cortez' army and the Aztecs' enemies conquered them and destroyed their civilisation.

An Aztec priest as a native would have painted him.

The Spanish went on to conquer all of Central America. They tried to wipe out all traces of its 'heathen' civilisations and convert it to Christianity. Instead of disappearing, many native traditions and beliefs simply changed form. For instance, the church of Mexico's patron saint, the Virgin of Guadeloupe, stands on the site of the Aztec mother goddess's temple.

Frida Kahlo's ancestors also came from Europe, including Spain. Much of Mexico's history was based on the gulf between the European upper classes and the native peasants. Wealthy landowners and miners lorded over dispossessed peasants, who sometimes turned to banditry.

A Spanish Conquistador (conqueror) as a Spaniard would have painted him.

After Mexico gained independence from Spain in 1821, its greatest challenge was to shape a country that respected all its peoples. It was pulled in many directions by conservative landowners, liberal reformers, peasant rebels and the Catholic Church. Its history is studded with civil wars and revolutions. Despite such conflicts, Mexican culture has become a rich blend of native and European traditions.

THE WORLD OF AN ARTIST

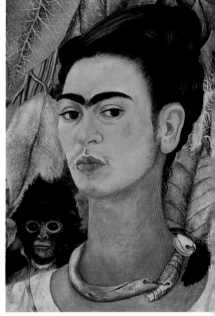

Through their work, artists share what is important to them. In the past, most Mexican art had been religious. Mexico entered the twentieth century with a revolution. Now art was to serve a new purpose. The country's leaders turned to artists and intellectuals like Frida Kahlo and Diego Rivera to help give Mexicans a sense of unity and pride.

Diego Rivera's art expresses his political beliefs. He painted huge murals to teach Mexicans about their history and destiny. He and other artists had to defend their paintings from those who disagreed with them, sometimes with pistols.

Frida painted about her feelings. Proud of her mixed heritage, she used images from both native and European traditions. She painted the Mexican landscape, full of contrasts between desert and jungle. She also used images of her pets – her dogs, birds, monkeys and little deer were like her children.

A self-portrait Frida Kahlo painted in 1938.

Frida created some strange and frightening paintings, which helped her express both her physical pain and her sense of belonging to two worlds that were often in conflict. Mexicans could identify with Frida's feelings of struggle, just as they could understand the huge message murals of her husband.

Europeans believe that Frida Kahlo's paintings belong to a style of art called Surrealism. But she was not influenced by anyone's style, though her friends included people like the famous artist Pablo Picasso.

Sometimes she influenced others, though. One European fashion designer, Elsa Schiaparelli, used Mexican themes for her gowns after meeting Frida. I can imagine Frida Kahlo, glamorous and intense, standing by some wide city street, while cars screech to a halt. She is like a vision from another world, a world where past and future, art and life join together.

MEXICO, LAND OF CONTRASTS

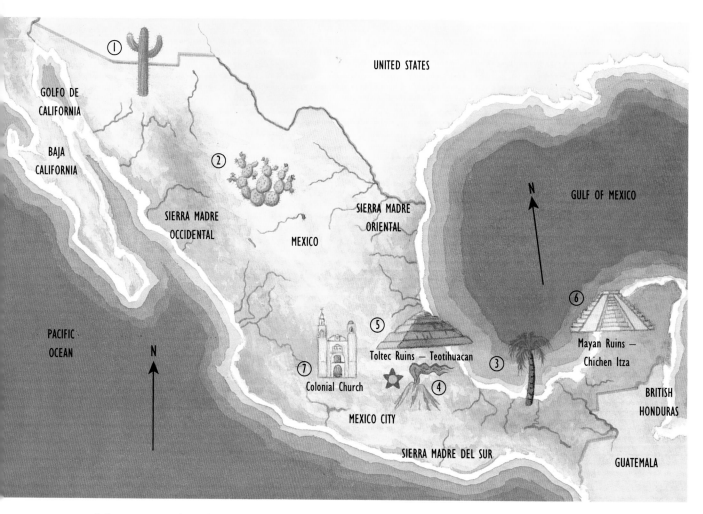

1. Saquaro cactus — desert plant.

2. Prickly pear cactus — desert plant.

3. Palm tree — tropical plant.

4. The volcano Popocateptl may have erupted just before Cortez arrived — it was seen as a warning by the Aztecs.

5. The Aztecs found these Toltec ruins at Teotihuacan — they believed they were where the world was born.

6. These Mayan ruins at Chichen Itza were buried in jungle for centuries.

7. The Spanish built colonial churches all over Mexico.

Further Reading

During my research for *Heroines* I consulted over 200 books. If you would like to know more about some of these heroines or their times, here is a list of books you might try. There are many wonderful biographies available for some heroines. Unfortunately, though, other heroines haven't been written about for young people yet, so adult books are all that are available. Books that are good for younger readers have an * beside them. Titles I particularly recommend have a ! beside them.

Agnodice
*Achterberg, Jeanne *Woman as Healer* Shambhala Publications, Boston 1990
*Peach, Susan and Millard, Anne *Usborne Illustrated World History: The Greeks* London 1990

Lady Murasaki Shikibu
Murasaki, Shikibu *The Tale of Genji* Knopf, New York 1992
Reischauer, Edwin and Fairbank, John *East Asia, the Great Tradition* Houghton Mifflin, Boston 1960
*Smith, Bradley *Japan: A History in Art* Doubleday, New York 1964

Eleanor of Aquitaine
*!Brooks, Polly Schoyer *Queen Eleanor, Independent Spirit of the Medieval World* Lippincott, New York 1983
*Meade, Marion *Eleanor of Aquitaine* Hawthorne Dutton, New York 1977

Joan of Arc
*!Brooks, Polly Schoyer *Beyond the Myth: the Story of Joan of Arc* Lippincott, New York 1990
*Dumarche, Lionel and Poussel, Jean *The Hundred Years War* Evans Brothers, London 1993
*!Williams, Jay *Joan of Arc* American Heritage Publishing Co (distributed by Harper & Row) New York 1963

Queen Elizabeth I
* Ross, Stewart *Elizabethan Life* Batsford, London 1991
Williams, Neville *All the Queen's Men* Weidenfeld & Nicholson, London 1972
The illustrations in this book are great, although the text is quite academic.
Williams, Neville *Elizabeth, Queen of England* Weidenfeld & Nicholson, London 1967

Sacajawea
Waldo, Anna Lee *Sacajawea* Avon, New York 1978
This is a fictionalised account of Sacajawea's life, based on years of research.
Frazier, Neta Lohnes *Sacajawea, the Girl Nobody Knows* David McKay, New York 1967
*Ballantine, Betty and Ian (Eds.) *The Native Americans, An Illustrated History* Turner Publishing, Atlanta, 1993
Thomas, Davis and Ponnefeldt, Karin (Eds.) *People of the First Man: Life Among the Plains Indians in their Final Days of Glory* Dutton, New York 1976
This book has some wonderful water-colours.

Harriet Tubman
*Adler, David *A Picture Book of Harriet Tubman* Holiday House, New York 1992

*!Taylor, M.W. *Harriet Tubman, Antislavery Activist* Chelsea House Publishers, New York 1991

Marie Curie
*Curie, Eve *Madame Curie: A Biography* Garden City Publications, New York 1943
*McKown, Robin *Marie Curie* Putnam, New York 1971
* Parker, Steve *Marie Curie and Radium* Belitha Press, London 1992
Reid, Robert *Marie Curie* Saturday Review Press, New York 1974

Anna Akhmatova
*Beriozkina, Patricia *Anna Akhmatova and her Circle* University of Arkansas Press, Fayetteville, 1994
Translated from Russian, this book has a real flavour of the language.
Reecler, Roberta *Anna Akhmatova, Poet and Prophet* St Martin's Press, New York 1994
*McAuley, Martin *The Stalin Files* Batsford, London 1979
*!Gibson, Michael *Russia Under Stalin* Wayland, London 1972

Madame Sun Yat-Sen
Chang, Jung *Wild Swans: Three Daughters of China* Flamingo, London 1993
Reischauer, Edwin, Fairbank, John and Craig, Albert *East Asia: The Modern Transformation* Houghton Mifflin, Boston 1965
Snow, Edgar *Red Star Over China* Gollancz, London 1968

Amelia Earhart
Goerner, Fred *The Search for Amelia Earhart* Doubleday, New York 1966
*!Lauber, Patricia *Lost Star: The Story of Amelia Earhart* Scholastic Press, New York 1988
Lovell, Mary *The Sound of Wings: The Biography of Amelia Earhart* Hutchinson, London 1989

Frida Kahlo Y Rivera
*Blacker, Irwin *Cortez and the Aztec Conquest* American Heritage Publications (distributed by Harper & Row), New York 1965
Cumberland, Charles Curtis *Mexico: The Struggle for Modernity* Oxford University Press, 1968
Herrera, Hayden *Frida* Harper & Row, New York 1983
*!Herrera, Hayden *Frida Kahlo: The Paintings* Harper & Row, New York 1993

General
Miles, Rosalind *The Women's History of the World*, Michael Joseph, London 1988
Rose, Phyllis (Ed) *Penguin Book of Women's Lives*, Viking, London 1994